Funny Bone

by Christopher Stitt

illustrated by Nathan Jurevicius

The Characters

Zack

Dad

Grandpa

James

The Setting

CONTENTS

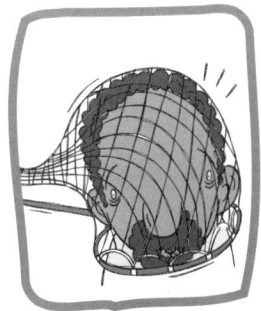

I've lost my funny bone

My dad took me to the circus.
He thought the clowns
were really funny.

He laughed so hard
he started to snort.

"Stop it, Dad," I said.

Dad rolled around laughing
and snorting. He slapped my back
and sent my popcorn flying.
I was really cross.

"What's wrong, Zack?
Lost your funny bone?" he laughed.

Can you lose your funny bone?
Had I really lost my funny bone?

6

Clowns are supposed to be funny.
I just couldn't laugh.

Where had my funny bone gone?
Was it hiding?
What did it look like?
How could I find it
if I didn't know what it looked
like?

8

I worried all the way home.

Dad chuckled to himself
for the whole trip.
"That clown was so funny!"

9

CHAPTER 2

Was it hiding?

I tried to work out
where my funny bone might hide.
My big sister, Sarah,
was watching TV.
Her silly laughter was starting
to annoy me.

"This is the funniest show
I've ever seen. What do you think,
Zack?"

I didn't laugh. I just got up
and left.

"What's wrong, Zack?
Lost your funny bone?"

Even Sarah knew I had lost
my funny bone.

I went to my room
and searched for my funny bone.

I searched under the bed.
It wasn't there. I searched
in the wardrobe.
There wasn't any room in there.

I searched in the toy box.
No luck at all.
I searched the dirty clothes basket.
Nothing would hide in there.

I lay awake all night.

CHAPTER 3

What does it look like?

The next day,
I went to the library.
I wanted to find a picture
of a funny bone.
It would be easier to find
if I knew what it looked like.

It was no use.
I couldn't find a picture anywhere.

17

I guessed that a funny bone
would look quite odd.

It had to be funny
and do silly things.

A funny bone would laugh a lot.
Maybe I would hear it.

My friend, James, came over.

"What are you doing, Zack?"

"Looking for something," I said.

"I hope it's your funny bone," said James.

"How did you know?"

"You must have lost it.
You were the only one
who didn't laugh at the puppet show
this morning."

I felt so bad.
Even my friends had noticed
that my funny bone was gone.

I had to set a trap to catch it.

CHAPTER 4

It's not funny!

That night, my grandpa
came for dinner.
He always tells jokes.

26

I didn't listen. I was too worried.

"What's wrong, Zack?
You always laugh at my jokes.
Lost your funny bone?"

"Yes! I have!" I yelled.

I ran up to my room
and slammed the door.

"I've got to catch
that funny bone," I thought.

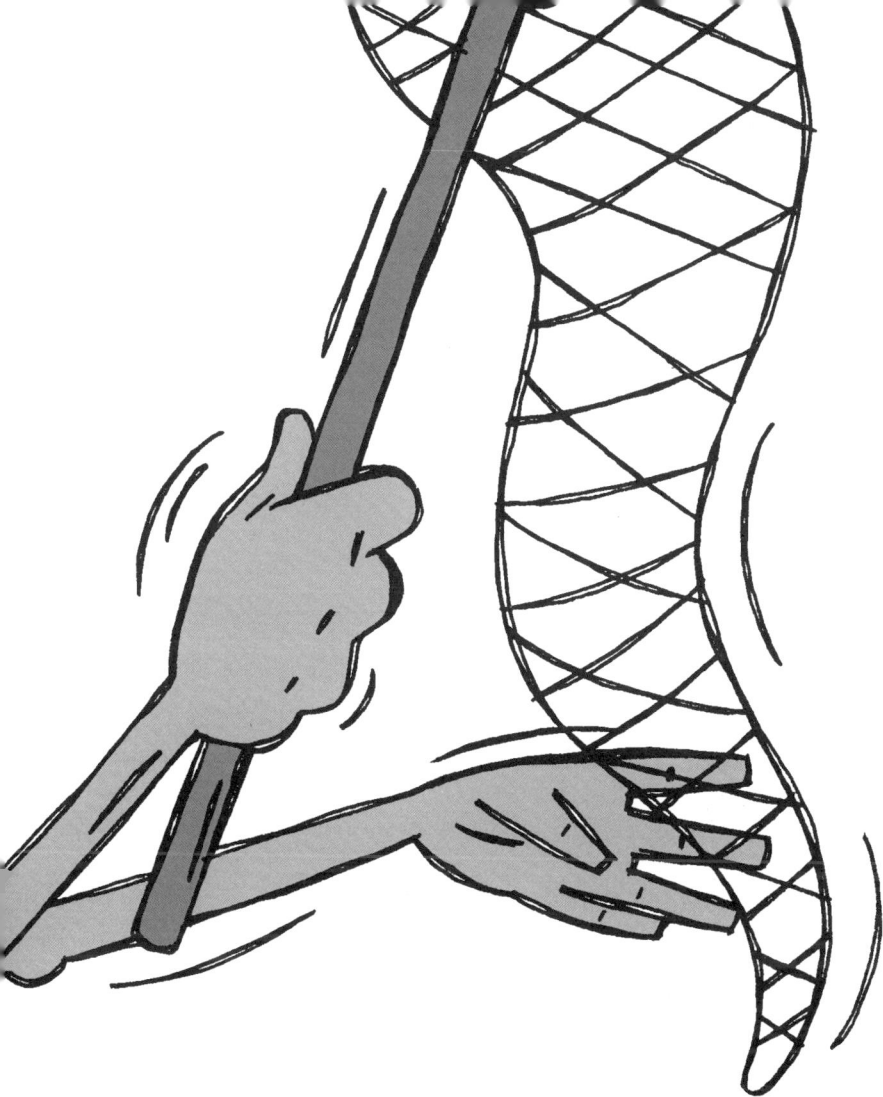

I needed my large net
for this job.

31

CHAPTER 5

Hunting a funny bone

I searched the house
from top to bottom.

When I went into the kitchen
I heard a funny noise.

"Hah hah hah snort ... hah hah hah
snort ... hah hah hah snort ..."

Who was laughing?
Maybe it was my funny bone?
It sounded like a funny bone.

I lifted my net.
I brought it down fast and hard.
I caught my funny bone.

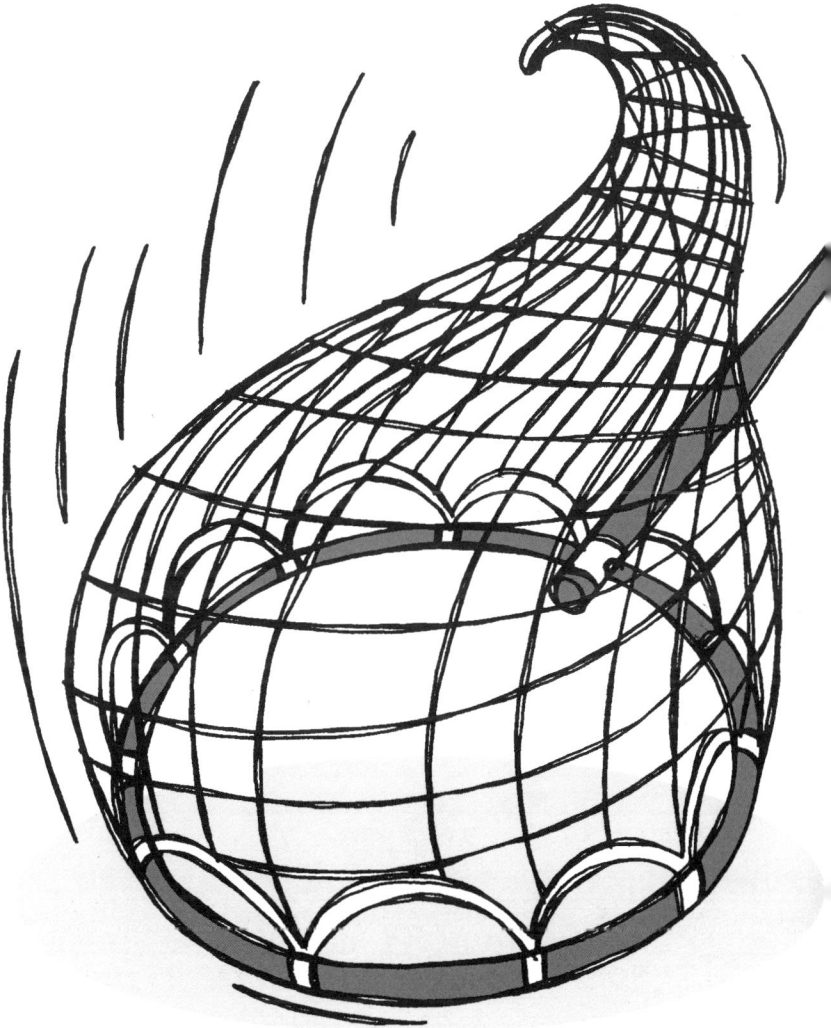

Well, I thought I did.
It was really my dad.

36

He wasn't laughing anymore.
He looked silly with my net
over his head.

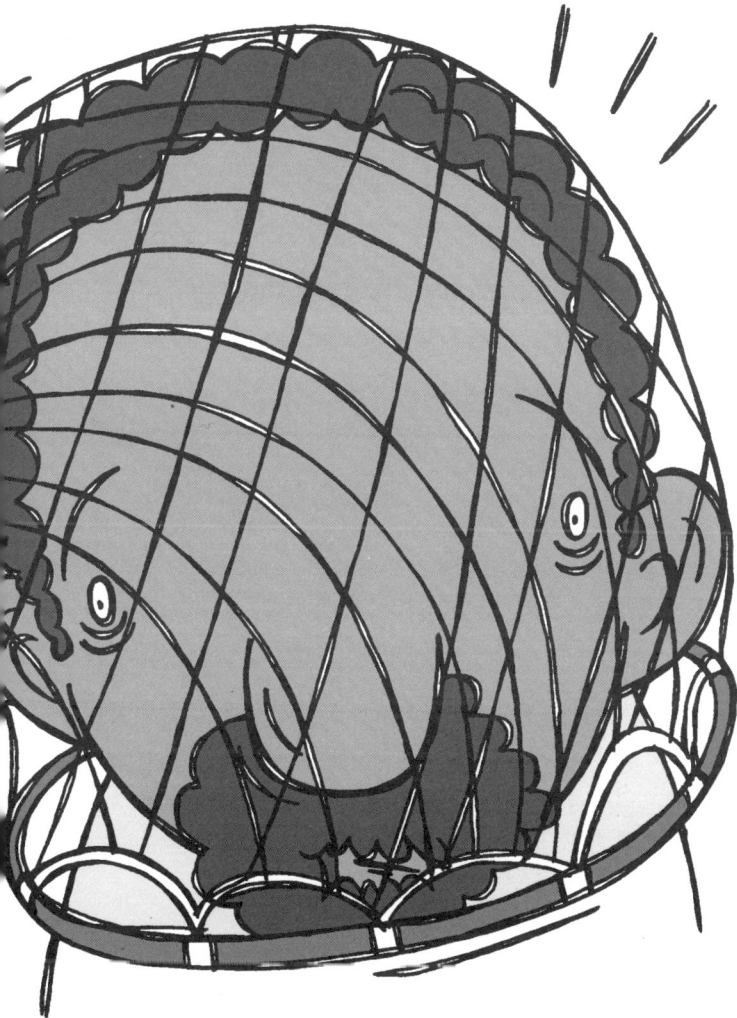

I felt a small rumble
in my tummy.

It began to bubble up inside me.
Then it burst out
in a flood of laughter.
I hadn't laughed this hard in ages.

39

Dad didn't laugh. He just struggled
to get the net off.

"I found my funny bone," I laughed.

Either that or I found my dad's.

41

GLOSSARY

circus
a big fair

embarrassed
felt self-conscious

magnifying
making things look bigger

rumble
a low thundery noise

snort
breathe noisily through your nose

searched
looked hard for something

worried
very anxious

struggled
made a big effort

Christopher Stitt

How high can you jump?

Not as high as I wish I could.

Why do ants have 6 legs?

They couldn't carry such heavy loads if they only had 4 legs.

What is your favourite toy?

My favourite toys as a kid were my animals.

(I wanted to be a zoo keeper.)

What is the hardest part of your day?

Getting up. I'm a bit of an owl. I write some of my best stories late at night.

Nathan Jurevicius

How high can you jump?

When I see a spider — very high!

Why do ants have 6 legs?

They need 2 to eat with, 2 to dance with and 2 to scratch with.

What is your favourite toy?

My new baby.

What is the hardest part of your day?

Choosing which herbal tea to drink at lunchtime.